LIVE OR DIE

Books by Anne Sexton

To Bedlam and Part Way Back
All My Pretty Ones
Live or Die

LIVE
OR
DIE

ANNE SEXTON

HOUGHTON MIFFLIN COMPANY BOSTON

W 20 19 18 17 16 15 14 13 12 11 10 9

Library of Congress Catalog Card Number: 66-22961
ISBN: 0-395-08180-7
Printed in the United States of America

For Max and Fred . . .

who made me an honorary *landsman.*

With one long breath, caught and held
in his chest, he fought his sadness over
his solitary life. Don't cry, you idiot!
Live or die, but don't poison everything . . .

from an early draft of *Herzog*
by Saul Bellow

ACKNOWLEDGMENTS

I would like to thank The American Academy of Arts and Letters for their Traveling Fellowship from June 1963 through June 1964 and the editors of the following magazines for their permission to reprint the following poems:

The *Carleton Miscellany*: And One for My Dame, Consorting with Angels
Critical Quarterly (England): Those Times . . . , Christmas Eve
Encounter (England): Walking in Paris
Harper's Magazine: Mother and Jack and the Rain, For the Year of the Insane, Love Song
The *Hudson Review*: Imitations of Drowning, To Lose the Earth, Crossing the Atlantic, Menstruation at Forty, Two Sons
The *New Yorker*: The Sun; Three Green Windows; Little Girl, My Stringbean, My Lovely Woman; Your Face on the Dog's Neck; Pain for a Daughter
The *Observer* (England) (18 October 1964): Wanting to Die
Poetry: Somewhere in Africa, KE 6–8018, The Wedding Night, Sylvia's Death
The *Sewanee Review*: The Legend of the One-eyed Man
Tri-Quarterly: Suicide Note, The Addict, Protestant Easter, Man and Wife, Cripples and Other Stories, Live

AUTHOR'S NOTE

To begin with, I have placed these poems (1962–1966) in the order in which they were written with all due apologies for the fact that they read like a fever chart for a bad case of melancholy. But I thought the order of their creation might be of interest to some readers, and, as André Gide wrote in his journal, "Despite every resolution of optimism, melancholy occasionally wins out: man has decidedly botched up the planet."

ANNE SEXTON

CONTENTS

LIVE OR DIE

AND ONE FOR MY DAME

A born salesman,
my father made all his dough
by selling wool to Fieldcrest, Woolrich and Faribo.

A born talker,
he could sell one hundred wet-down bales
of that white stuff. He could clock the miles and sales

and make it pay.
At home each sentence he would utter
had first pleased the buyer who'd paid him off in butter.

Each word
had been tried over and over, at any rate,
on the man who was sold by the man who filled my plate.

My father hovered
over the Yorkshire pudding and the beef:
a peddler, a hawker, a merchant and an Indian chief.

Roosevelt! Willkie! and war!
How suddenly gauche I was
with my old-maid heart and my funny teenage applause.

Each night at home
my father was in love with maps
while the radio fought its battles with Nazis and Japs.

Except when he hid
in his bedroom on a three-day drunk,
he typed out complex itineraries, packed his trunk,

1

his matched luggage
and pocketed a confirmed reservation,
his heart already pushing over the red routes of the nation.

I sit at my desk
each night with no place to go,
opening the wrinkled maps of Milwaukee and Buffalo,

the whole U.S.,
its cemeteries, its arbitrary time zones,
through routes like small veins, capitals like small stones.

He died on the road,
his heart pushed from neck to back,
his white hanky signaling from the window of the Cadillac.

My husband,
as blue-eyed as a picture book, sells wool:
boxes of card waste, laps and rovings he can pull

to the thread
and say *Leicester, Rambouillet, Merino,*
a half-blood, it's greasy and thick, yellow as old snow.

And when you drive off, my darling,
Yes, sir! Yes, sir! It's one for my dame,
your sample cases branded with my father's name,

your itinerary open,
its tolls ticking and greedy,
its highways built up like new loves, raw and speedy.

January 25, 1962

THE SUN

I have heard of fish
coming up for the sun
who stayed forever,
shoulder to shoulder,
avenues of fish that never got back,
all their proud spots and solitudes
sucked out of them.

I think of flies
who come from their foul caves
out into the arena.
They are transparent at first.
Then they are blue with copper wings.
They glitter on the foreheads of men.
Neither bird nor acrobat
they will dry out like small black shoes.

I am an identical being.
Diseased by the cold and the smell of the house
I undress under the burning magnifying glass.
My skin flattens out like sea water.
O yellow eye,
let me be sick with your heat,
let me be feverish and frowning.
Now I am utterly given.
I am your daughter, your sweet-meat,
your priest, your mouth and your bird
and I will tell them all stories of you
until I am laid away forever,
a thin gray banner.

May 1962

FLEE ON YOUR DONKEY

Ma faim, Anne, Anne,
Fuis sur ton âne . . . Rimbaud

Because there was no other place
to flee to,
I came back to the scene of the disordered senses,
came back last night at midnight,
arriving in the thick June night
without luggage or defenses,
giving up my car keys and my cash,
keeping only a pack of Salem cigarettes
the way a child holds on to a toy.
I signed myself in where a stranger
puts the inked-in X's —
for this is a mental hospital,
not a child's game.

Today an interne knocks my knees,
testing for reflexes.
Once I would have winked and begged for dope.
Today I am terribly patient.
Today crows play black-jack
on the stethoscope.

Everyone has left me
except my muse,
that good nurse.
She stays in my hand,
a mild white mouse.

The curtains, lazy and delicate,
billow and flutter and drop
like the Victorian skirts

4

of my two maiden aunts
who kept an antique shop.

Hornets have been sent.
They cluster like floral arrangements on the screen.
Hornets, dragging their thin stingers,
hover outside, all knowing,
hissing: *the hornet knows.*
I heard it as a child
but what was it that he meant?
The hornet knows!
What happened to Jack and Doc and Reggy?
Who remembers what lurks in the heart of man?
What did The Green Hornet mean, *he knows?*
Or have I got it wrong?
Is it The Shadow who had seen
me from my bedside radio?

Now it's *Dinn, Dinn, Dinn!*
while the ladies in the next room argue
and pick their teeth.
Upstairs a girl curls like a snail;
in another room someone tries to eat a shoe;
meanwhile an adolescent pads up and down
the hall in his white tennis socks.
A new doctor makes rounds
advertising tranquilizers, insulin, or shock
to the uninitiated.

Six years of such small preoccupations!
Six years of shuttling in and out of this place!
O my hunger! My hunger!
I could have gone around the world twice
or had new children — all boys.
It was a long trip with little days in it
and no new places.

5

In here,
it's the same old crowd,
the same ruined scene.
The alcoholic arrives with his golf clubs.
The suicide arrives with extra pills sewn
into the lining of her dress.
The permanent guests have done nothing new.
Their faces are still small
like babies with jaundice.

Meanwhile,
they carried out my mother,
wrapped like somebody's doll, in sheets,
bandaged her jaw and stuffed up her holes.
My father, too. He went out on the rotten blood
he used up on other women in the Middle West.
He went out, a cured old alcoholic
on crooked feet and useless hands.
He went out calling for his father
who died all by himself long ago —
that fat banker who got locked up,
his genes suspended like dollars,
wrapped up in his secret,
tied up securely in a straitjacket.

But you, my doctor, my enthusiast,
were better than Christ;
you promised me another world
to tell me who
I was.

I spent most of my time,
a stranger,
damned and in trance — that little hut,
that naked blue-veined place,
my eyes shut on the confusing office,

eyes circling into my childhood,
eyes newly cut.
Years of hints
strung out — a serialized case history —
thirty-three years of the same dull incest
that sustained us both.
You, my bachelor analyst,
who sat on Marlborough Street,
sharing your office with your mother
and giving up cigarettes each New Year,
were the new God,
the manager of the Gideon Bible.

I was your third-grader
with a blue star on my forehead.
In trance I could be any age,
voice, gesture — all turned backward
like a drugstore clock.
Awake, I memorized dreams.
Dreams came into the ring
like third string fighters,
each one a bad bet
who might win
because there was no other.

I stared at them,
concentrating on the abyss
the way one looks down into a rock quarry,
uncountable miles down,
my hands swinging down like hooks
to pull dreams up out of their cage.
O my hunger! My hunger!

Once,
outside your office,
I collapsed in the old-fashioned swoon
between the illegally parked cars.

I threw myself down,
pretending dead for eight hours.
I thought I had died
into a snowstorm.
Above my head
chains cracked along like teeth
digging their way through the snowy street.
I lay there
like an overcoat
that someone had thrown away.
You carried me back in,
awkwardly, tenderly,
with the help of the red-haired secretary
who was built like a lifeguard.
My shoes,
I remember,
were lost in the snowbank
as if I planned never to walk again.

That was the winter
that my mother died,
half mad on morphine,
blown up, at last,
like a pregnant pig.
I was her dreamy evil eye.
In fact,
I carried a knife in my pocketbook —
my husband's good L. L. Bean hunting knife.
I wasn't sure if I should slash a tire
or scrape the guts out of some dream.

You taught me
to believe in dreams;
thus I was the dredger.
I held them like an old woman with arthritic fingers,
carefully straining the water out —

sweet dark playthings,
and above all, mysterious
until they grew mournful and weak.
O my hunger! My hunger!
I was the one
who opened the warm eyelid
like a surgeon
and brought forth young girls
to grunt like fish.

I told you,
I said —
but I was lying —
that the knife was for my mother . . .
and then I delivered her.

The curtains flutter out
and slump against the bars.
They are my two thin ladies
named Blanche and Rose.
The grounds outside
are pruned like an estate at Newport.
Far off, in the field,
something yellow grows.

Was it last month or last year
that the ambulance ran like a hearse
with its siren blowing on suicide —
Dinn, dinn, dinn! —
a noon whistle that kept insisting on life
all the way through the traffic lights?

I have come back
but disorder is not what it was.
I have lost the trick of it!
The innocence of it!

That fellow-patient in his stovepipe hat
with his fiery joke, his manic smile —
even he seems blurred, small and pale.
I have come back,
recommitted,
fastened to the wall like a bathroom plunger,
held like a prisoner
who was so poor
he fell in love with jail.

I stand at this old window
complaining of the soup,
examining the grounds,
allowing myself the wasted life.
Soon I will raise my face for a white flag,
and when God enters the fort,
I won't spit or gag on his finger.
I will eat it like a white flower.
Is this the old trick, the wasting away,
the skull that waits for its dose
of electric power?

This is madness
but a kind of hunger.
What good are my questions
in this hierarchy of death
where the earth and the stones go
Dinn! Dinn! Dinn!
It is hardly a feast.
It is my stomach that makes me suffer.

Turn, my hungers!
For once make a deliberate decision.
There are brains that rot here
like black bananas.
Hearts have grown as flat as dinner plates.

Anne, Anne,
flee on your donkey,
flee this sad hotel,
ride out on some hairy beast,
gallop backward pressing
your buttocks to his withers,
sit to his clumsy gait somehow.
Ride out
any old way you please!
In this place everyone talks to his own mouth.
That's what it means to be crazy.
Those I loved best died of it —
the fool's disease.

June 1962

THREE GREEN WINDOWS

Half awake in my Sunday nap
I see three green windows
in three different lights —
one west, one south, one east.
I have forgotten that old friends are dying.
I have forgotten that I grow middle-aged.
At each window such rustlings!
The trees persist, yeasty and sensuous,
as thick as saints.
I see three wet gargoyles covered with birds.
Their skins shine in the sun like leather.

I'm on my bed as light as a sponge.
Soon it will be summer.
She is my mother.
She will tell me a story and keep me asleep
against her plump and fruity skin.
I see leaves —
leaves that are washed and innocent,
leaves that never knew a cellar,
born in their own green blood
like the hands of mermaids.

I do not think of the rusty wagon on the walk.
I pay no attention to the red squirrels
that leap like machines beside the house.
I do not remember the real trunks of the trees
that stand beneath the windows
as bulky as artichokes.
I turn like a giant,

secretly watching, secretly knowing,
secretly naming each elegant sea.

I have misplaced the Van Allen belt,
the sewers and the drainage,
the urban renewal and the suburban centers.
I have forgotten the names of the literary critics.
I know what I know.
I am the child I was,
living the life that was mine.
I am young and half asleep.
It is a time of water, a time of trees.

June 1962

SOMEWHERE IN AFRICA

Must you leave, John Holmes, with the prayers and psalms
you never said, said over you? Death with no rage
to weigh you down? Praised by the mild God, his arm
over the pulpit, leaving you timid, with no real age,

whitewashed by belief, as dull as the windy preacher!
Dead of a dark thing, John Holmes, you've been lost
in the college chapel, mourned as father and teacher,
mourned with piety and grace under the University Cross.

Your last book unsung, your last hard words unknown,
abandoned by science, cancer blossomed in your throat,
rooted like bougainvillea into your gray backbone,
ruptured your pores until you wore it like a coat.

The thick petals, the exotic reds, the purples and whites
covered up your nakedness and bore you up with all
their blind power. I think of your last June nights
in Boston, your body swollen but light, your eyes small

as you let the nurses carry you into a strange land.
. . . If this is death and God is necessary let him be hidden
from the missionary, the well-wisher and the glad hand.
Let God be some tribal female who is known but forbidden.

Let there be this God who is a woman who will place you
upon her shallow boat, who is a woman naked to the waist,
moist with palm oil and sweat, a woman of some virtue
and wild breasts, her limbs excellent, unbruised and chaste.

14

Let her take you. She will put twelve strong men at the oars
for you are stronger than mahogany and your bones fill
the boat high as with fruit and bark from the interior.
She will have you now, you whom the funeral cannot kill.

John Holmes, cut from a single tree, lie heavy in her hold
and go down that river with the ivory, the copra and the gold.

July 1, 1962

IMITATIONS OF DROWNING

Fear
of drowning,
fear of being that alone,
kept me busy making a deal
as if I could buy
my way out of it
and it worked for two years
and all of July.

This August I began to dream of drowning. The dying
went on and on in water as white and clear
as the gin I drink each day at half-past five.
Going down for the last time, the last breath lying,
I grapple with eels like ropes — it's ether, it's queer
and then, at last, it's done. Now the scavengers arrive,
the hard crawlers who come to clean up the ocean floor.
And death, that old butcher, will bother me no more.

I
had never
had this dream before
except twice when my parents
clung to rafts
and sat together for death,
frozen
like lewd photographs.

Who listens to dreams? Only symbols for something —
like money for the analyst or your mother's wig,
the arm I almost lost in the washroom wringer,

following fear to its core, tugging the old string.
But real drowning is for someone else. It's too big
to put in your mouth on purpose, it puts hot stingers
in your tongue and vomit in your nose as your lungs break.
Tossed like a wet dog by that juggler, you die awake.

Fear,
a motor,
pumps me around and around
until I fade slowly
and the crowd laughs.
I fade out, an old bicycle rider
whose odds are measured
in actuary graphs.

This weekend the papers were black with the new highway
fatalities and in Boston the strangler found another victim
and we were all in Truro drinking beer and writing checks.
The others rode the surf, commanding rafts like sleighs.
I swam — but the tide came in like ten thousand orgasms.
I swam — but the waves were higher than horses' necks.
I was shut up in that closet, until, biting the door,
they dragged me out, dribbling urine on the gritty shore.

Breathe!
And you'll know . . .
an ant in a pot of chocolate,
it boils
and surrounds you.
There is no news in fear
but in the end it's fear
that drowns you.

September 1962

MOTHER AND JACK AND THE RAIN

I have a room of my own.
Rain drops onto it. Rain drops down like worms
from the trees onto my frontal bone.
Haunted, always haunted by rain, the room affirms
the words that I will make alone.
I come like the blind feeling for shelves,
feeling for wood as hard as an apple,
fingering the pen lightly, my blade.
With this pen I take in hand my selves
and with these dead disciples I will grapple.
Though rain curses the window
let the poem be made.

Rain is a finger on my eyeball.
Rain drills in with its old unnecessary stories . . .
I went to bed like a horse to its stall.
On my damp summer bed I cradled my salty knees
and heard father kiss me through the wall
and heard mother's heart pump like the tides.
The fog horn flattened the sea into leather.
I made no voyages, I owned no passport.
I was the daughter. Whiskey fortified
my father in the next room. He outlasted the weather,
counted his booty and brought
his ship into port.

Rain, rain, at sixteen
where I lay all night with Jack beside a tiny lake
and did nothing at all, lay as straight as a bean.
We played bridge and beer games for their own sake,

filled up the lamp with kerosene,
brushed our teeth, made sandwiches and tea
and lay down on the cabin bed to sleep.
I lay, a blind lake, feigning sleep while Jack
pulled back the wooly covers to see
my body, that invisible body that girls keep.
All that sweet night we rode out
the storm back to back.

Now Jack says the Mass
and mother died using her own bones for crutches.
There is rain on the wood, rain on the glass
and I'm in a room of my own. I think too much.
Fish swim from the eyes of God. Let them pass.
Mother and Jack fill up heaven; they endorse
my womanhood. Near land my ship comes about.
I come to this land to ride my horse,
to try my own guitar, to copy out
their two separate names like sunflowers, to conjure
up my daily bread, to endure,
somehow to endure.

October 1962

CONSORTING WITH ANGELS

I was tired of being a woman,
tired of the spoons and the pots,
tired of my mouth and my breasts,
tired of the cosmetics and the silks.
There were still men who sat at my table,
circled around the bowl I offered up.
The bowl was filled with purple grapes
and the flies hovered in for the scent
and even my father came with his white bone.
But I was tired of the gender of things.

Last night I had a dream
and I said to it . . .
"You are the answer.
You will outlive my husband and my father."
In that dream there was a city made of chains
where Joan was put to death in man's clothes
and the nature of the angels went unexplained,
no two made in the same species,
one with a nose, one with an ear in its hand,
one chewing a star and recording its orbit,
each one like a poem obeying itself,
performing God's functions,
a people apart.

"You are the answer,"
I said, and entered,
lying down on the gates of the city.
Then the chains were fastened around me
and I lost my common gender and my final aspect.

Adam was on the left of me
and Eve was on the right of me,
both thoroughly inconsistent with the world of reason.
We wove our arms together
and rode under the sun.
I was not a woman anymore,
not one thing or the other.

O daughters of Jerusalem,
the king has brought me into his chamber.
I am black and I am beautiful.
I've been opened and undressed.
I have no arms or legs.
I'm all one skin like a fish.
I'm no more a woman
than Christ was a man.

February 1963

THE LEGEND OF THE ONE-EYED MAN

Like Oedipus I am losing my sight.
Like Judas I have done my wrong.
Their punishment is over;
the shame and disgrace of it
are all used up.
But as for me,
look into my face
and you will know that crimes dropped upon me
as from a high building
and although I cannot speak of them
or explain the degrading details
I have remembered much
about Judas —
about Judas, the old and the famous —
that you overlooked.

The story of his life
is the story of mine.
I have one glass eye.
My nerves push against its painted surface
but the other one
waiting for judgment
continues to see . . .

Of course
the New Testament is very small.
Its mouth opens four times —
as out-of-date as a prehistoric monster,
yet somehow man-made,
held together by pullies

like the stone jaw of a back-hoe.
It gouges out the Judaic ground,
taking its own backyard
like a virgin daughter.

And furthermore how did Judas come into it —
that Judas Iscariot,
belonging to the tribe of Reuben?
He should have tried to lift him up there!
His neck like an iron pole,
hard as Newcastle,
his heart as stiff as beeswax,
his legs swollen and unmarked,
his other limbs still growing.
All of it heavy!
That dead weight that would have been his fault.
He should have known!

In the first place who builds up such ugliness?
I think of this man saying . . .
Look! Here's the price to do it
plus the cost of the raw materials
and if it took him three or four days
to do it, then, they'd understand.
They figured the boards in excess
of three hundred pounds.
They figured it weighed enough
to support a man. They said,
fifteen stone is the approximate weight
of a thief.

Its ugliness is a matter of custom.
If there was a mistake made
then the Crucifix was constructed wrong . . .
not from the quality of the pine,
not from hanging a mirror,

not from dropping the studding or the drill
but from having an inspiration.
But Judas was not a genius
or under the auspices of an inspiration.

I don't know whether it was gold or silver.
I don't know why he betrayed him
other than his motives,
other than the avaricious and dishonest man.
And then there were the forbidden crimes,
those that were expressly foretold,
and then overlooked
and then forgotten
except by me . . .
Judas had a mother
just as I had a mother.
Oh! Honor and relish the facts!
Do not think of the intense sensation
I have as I tell you this
but think only. . .

Judas had a mother.
His mother had a dream.
Because of this dream
he was altogether managed by fate
and thus he raped her.
As a crime we hear little of this.
Also he sold his God.

March 1963

LOVE SONG

I was
the girl of the chain letter,
the girl full of talk of coffins and keyholes,
the one of the telephone bills,
the wrinkled photo and the lost connections,
the one who kept saying —
Listen! Listen!
We must never! We must never!
and all those things . . .

the one
with her eyes half under her coat,
with her large gun-metal blue eyes,
with the thin vein at the bend of her neck
that hummed like a tuning fork,
with her shoulders as bare as a building,
with her thin foot and her thin toes,
with an old red hook in her mouth,
the mouth that kept bleeding
into the terrible fields of her soul . . .

the one
who kept dropping off to sleep,
as old as a stone she was,
each hand like a piece of cement,
for hours and hours
and then she'd wake,
after the small death,
and then she'd be as soft as,
as delicate as . . .

as soft and delicate as
an excess of light,
with nothing dangerous at all,
like a beggar who eats
or a mouse on a rooftop
with no trap doors,
with nothing more honest
than your hand in her hand —
with nobody, nobody but you!
and all those things.
nobody, nobody but you!
Oh! There is no translating
that ocean,
that music,
that theater,
that field of ponies.

April 19, 1963

MAN AND WIFE

*To speke of wo
    that is in mariage . . .*

We are not lovers.
We do not even know each other.
We look alike
but we have nothing to say.
We are like pigeons . . .

that pair who came to the suburbs
by mistake,
forsaking Boston where they bumped
their small heads against a blind wall,
having worn out the fruit stalls in the North End,
the amethyst windows of Louisburg Square,
the seats on the Common
And the traffic that kept stamping
and stamping.

Now there is green rain for everyone
as common as eyewash.
Now they are together
like strangers in a two-seater outhouse,
eating and squatting together.
They have teeth and knees
but they do not speak.
A soldier is forced to stay with a soldier
because they share the same dirt
and the same blows.

They are exiles
soiled by the same sweat and the drunkard's dream.
As it is they can only hang on,
their red claws wound like bracelets
around the same limb.
Even their song is not a sure thing.
It is not a language;
it is a kind of breathing.
They are two asthmatics
whose breath sobs in and out
through a small fuzzy pipe.

Like them
we neither talk nor clear our throats.
Oh darling,
we gasp in unison beside our window pane,
drunk on the drunkard's dream.
Like them
we can only hang on.

But they would pierce our heart
if they could only fly the distance.

May 1963

THOSE TIMES . . .

At six
I lived in a graveyard full of dolls,
avoiding myself,
my body, the suspect
in its grotesque house.
I was locked in my room all day behind a gate,
a prison cell.
I was the exile
who sat all day in a knot.

I will speak of the little childhood cruelties,
being a third child,
the last given
and the last taken —
of the nightly humiliations when Mother undressed me,
of the life of the daytime, locked in my room —
being the unwanted, the mistake
that Mother used to keep Father
from his divorce.
Divorce!
The romantic's friend,
romantics who fly into maps
of other countries,
hips and noses and mountains,
into Asia or the Black Forest,
or caught by 1928,
the year of the *me*,
by mistake,
not for divorce
but instead.

The me who refused to suck on breasts
she couldn't please,
the me whose body grew unsurely,
the me who stepped on the noses of dolls
she couldn't break.
I think of the dolls,
so well made,
so perfectly put together
as I pressed them against me,
kissing their little imaginary mouths.
I remember their smooth skin,
those newly delivered,
the pink skin and the serious China-blue eyes.
They came from a mysterious country
without the pang of birth,
born quietly and well.
When I wanted to visit,
the closet is where I rehearsed my life,
all day among shoes,
away from the glare of the bulb in the ceiling,
away from the bed and the heavy table
and the same terrible rose repeating on the walls.

I did not question it.
I hid in the closet as one hides in a tree.

I grew into it like a root
and yet I planned such plans of flight,
believing I would take my body into the sky,
dragging it with me like a large bed.
And although I was unskilled
I was sure to get there or at least
to move up like an elevator.
With such dreams,
storing their energy like a bull,
I planned my growth and my womanhood
as one choreographs a dance.

I knew that if I waited among shoes
I was sure to outgrow them,
the heavy oxfords, the thick execution reds,
shoes that lay together like partners,
the sneakers thick with Griffin eyewash
and then the dresses swinging above me,
always above me, empty and sensible
with sashes and puffs,
with collars and two-inch hems
and evil fortunes in their belts.

I sat all day
stuffing my heart into a shoe box,
avoiding the precious window
as if it were an ugly eye
through which birds coughed,
chained to the heaving trees;
avoiding the wallpaper of the room
where tongues bloomed over and over,
bursting from lips like sea flowers —
and in this way I waited out the day
until my mother,
the large one,
came to force me to undress.

I lay there silently,
hoarding my small dignity.
I did not ask about the gate or the closet.
I did not question the bedtime ritual
where, on the cold bathroom tiles,
I was spread out daily
and examined for flaws.

I did not know
that my bones,
those solids, those pieces of sculpture
would not splinter.

I did not know the woman I would be
nor that blood would bloom in me
each month like an exotic flower,
nor that children,
two monuments,
would break from between my legs
two cramped girls breathing carelessly,
each asleep in her tiny beauty.
I did not know that my life, in the end,
would run over my mother's like a truck
and all that would remain
from the year I was six
was a small hole in my heart, a deaf spot,
so that I might hear
the unsaid more clearly.

June 1963

TWO SONS

Where and to whom
you are married I can only guess
in my piecemeal fashion. I grow old on my bitterness.

On the unique occasion
of your two sudden wedding days
I open some cheap wine, a tin of lobster and mayonnaise.

I sit in an old lady's room
where families used to feast
where the wind blows in like soot from north-northeast.

Both of you monopolized
with no real forwarding address
except for two silly postcards you bothered to send home,

one of them written in grease
as you undid her dress
in Mexico, the other airmailed to Boston from Rome

just before the small ceremony
at the American Church.
Both of you made of my cooking, those suppers of starch

and beef, and with my library,
my medicine, my bath water,
both sinking into small brown pools like muddy otters!

You make a toast for tomorrow
and smash the cup,
letting your false women lap the dish I had to fatten up.

When you come back I'll buy
a wig of yellow hair;
I'll squat in a new red dress; I'll be playing solitaire

on the kitchen floor.
Yes . . . I'll gather myself in
like cut flowers and ask you how you are and where you've been.

July 22, 1963

TO LOSE THE EARTH

*To lose the earth you know, for greater knowing; to lose
the life you have, for greater life; to leave the friends
you loved, for greater loving; to find a land more kind
than home, more large than earth . . . Thomas Wolfe*

The wreckage of Europe or the birth of Africa,
the old palaces, the wallets of the tourists,
the Common Market or the smart cafés,
the boulevards in the graceful evening,
the cliff-hangers, the scientists,
and the little shops raising their prices
mean nothing to me.
Each day I think only
of this place, only this place
where the musician works.
He plays his flute in a cave
that a pharaoh built by the sea.
He is blowing on light,
each time for the first time.
His fingers cover the mouths of all the sopranos,
each a princess in an exact position.

If you can find it,
the music takes place in a grotto,
a great hole in the earth.
You must wait outside the mouth hole for hours
while the Egyptian boatman howls the password
and the sea keeps booming and booming.
At that point you will be in a state of terror,
moaning, "How can we?"
for you will see only the unreliable chain
that is meant to drag you in.
It is called *Waiting on the Edge.*

At the moment of entry
your head will be below the gunwales,
your shoulders will rock and struggle
as you ship hogsheads of water.
"Here?" you will ask,
looking around for your camera and shoes
and then you will not need to ask
for the flutist is playing.
This is the music that you waited for
in the great concert halls,
season after season,
and never found.
It is called *Being Inside*.

It is close to being dead.
Although you had expected pain
there will be no pain,
only that piper, that midwife
with his unforgettable woman's face.
The left side of the flute cannot be seen.
It grows into the wall like something human.
It is driven into the wall like a pipe
that extends, some say,
into the sun.
The flutist sucks and blows.
He is both a woman
and a man,
abandoned to that great force
and spilling it back out.
He is the undefiled,
the eternal listener
who has cried back into the earth.

In the distance other travelers,
others like you who came out of simple curiosity,
remain for generations.

From all sides of the cave
you will notice the protruding fingernails
of the dead.
From their coffins
as stale as cheap cigars,
through the tons of suffocating dirt,
they heard
and dug down immediately and persistently.
They scratched down for centuries
in order to enter.

At the far right,
rising from an underground sea,
his toes curled on a black wave,
stands the dwarf;
his instrument is an extension of his tongue.
He holds it fast
as if it would get away,
wet and cold and slippery as it is.
He is the other half.
The one you hadn't expected.
You will jump up and point at him
shouting, "It is you!"
but he will not listen.
He plays his own song, cursing the wind
with his enormous misshapen mouth.

And you, having heard,
you will never leave.
At the moment of entry
you were fed —
— and then you knew.

January 1963

SYLVIA'S DEATH

for Sylvia Plath

O Sylvia, Sylvia,
with a dead box of stones and spoons,

with two children, two meteors
wandering loose in the tiny playroom,

with your mouth into the sheet,
into the roofbeam, into the dumb prayer,

(Sylvia, Sylvia,
where did you go
after you wrote me
from Devonshire
about raising potatoes
and keeping bees?)

what did you stand by,
just how did you lie down into?

Thief! —
how did you crawl into,

crawl down alone
into the death I wanted so badly and for so long,

the death we said we both outgrew,
the one we wore on our skinny breasts,

the one we talked of so often each time
we downed three extra dry martinis in Boston,

the death that talked of analysts and cures,
the death that talked like brides with plots,

the death we drank to,
the motives and then the quiet deed?

(In Boston
the dying
ride in cabs,
yes death again,
that ride home
with *our* boy.)

O Sylvia, I remember the sleepy drummer
who beat on our eyes with an old story,

how we wanted to let him come
like a sadist or a New York fairy

to do his job,
a necessity, a window in a wall or a crib,

and since that time he waited
under our heart, our cupboard,

and I see now that we store him up
year after year, old suicides

and I know at the news of your death,
a terrible taste for it, like salt.

(And me,
me too.
And now, Sylvia,
you again
with death again,
that ride home
with *our* boy.)

And I say only
with my arms stretched out into that stone place,

what is your death
but an old belonging,

a mole that fell out
of one of your poems?

(O friend,
while the moon's bad,
and the king's gone,
and the queen's at her wit's end
the bar fly ought to sing!)

O tiny mother,
you too!
O funny duchess!
O blonde thing!

February 17, 1963

PROTESTANT EASTER

eight years old

When he was a little boy
Jesus was good all the time.
No wonder that he grew up to be such a big shot
who could forgive people so much.
When he died everyone was mean.
Later on he rose when no one else was looking.
Either he was hiding or else
he went up.
Maybe he was only hiding?
Maybe he could fly?

Yesterday I found a purple crocus
blowing its way out of the snow.
It was all alone.
It was getting its work done.
Maybe Jesus was only getting his work done
and letting God blow him off the Cross
and maybe he was afraid for a minute
so he hid under the big stones.
He was smart to go to sleep up there
even though his mother got so sad
and let them put him in a cave.
I sat in a tunnel when I was five.
That tunnel, my mother said,
went straight into the big river
and so I never went again.
Maybe Jesus knew my tunnel

and crawled right through to the river
so he could wash all the blood off.
Maybe he only meant to get clean
and then come back again?
Don't tell me that he went up in smoke
like Daddy's cigar!
He didn't blow out like a match!

It is special
being here at Easter
with the Cross they built like a capital T.
The ceiling is an upside-down rowboat.
I usually count its ribs.
Maybe he was drowning?
Or maybe we are all upside down?
I can see the face of a mouse inside
of all that stained-glass window.
Well, it could be a mouse!
Once I thought the Bunny Rabbit was special
and I hunted for eggs.
That's when I was seven.
I'm grownup now. Now it's really Jesus.
I just have to get Him straight.
And right now.

Who are we anyhow?
What do we belong to?
Are we a *we?*
I think that he rose
but I'm not quite sure
and they don't really say
singing their *Alleluia*
in the churchy way.
Jesus was on that Cross.
After that they pounded nails into his hands.
After that, well, after that,

everyone wore hats
and then there was a big stone rolled away
and then almost everyone —
the ones who sit up straight —
looked at the ceiling.

Alleluia they sing.
They don't know.
They don't care if he was hiding or flying.
Well, it doesn't matter how he got there.
It matters where he was going.
The important thing for me
is that I'm wearing white gloves.
I always sit straight.
I keep on looking at the ceiling.
And about Jesus,
they couldn't be sure of it,
not so sure of it anyhow,
so they decided to become Protestants.
Those are the people that sing
when they aren't quite
sure.

Spring 1963

FOR THE YEAR OF THE INSANE

a prayer

O Mary, fragile mother,
hear me, hear me now
although I do not know your words.
The black rosary with its silver Christ
lies unblessed in my hand
for I am the unbeliever.
Each bead is round and hard between my fingers,
a small black angel.
O Mary, permit me this grace,
this crossing over,
although I am ugly,
submerged in my own past
and my own madness.
Although there are chairs
I lie on the floor.
Only my hands are alive,
touching beads.
Word for word, I stumble.
A beginner, I feel your mouth touch mine.

I count beads as waves,
hammering in upon me.
I am ill at their numbers,
sick, sick in the summer heat
and the window above me
is my only listener, my awkward being.
She is a large taker, a soother.

The giver of breath
she murmurs,
exhaling her wide lung like an enormous fish.

Closer and closer
comes the hour of my death
as I rearrange my face, grow back,
grow undeveloped and straight-haired.
All this is death.
In the mind there is a thin alley called death
and I move through it as
through water.
My body is useless.
It lies, curled like a dog on the carpet.
It has given up.
There are no words here except the half-learned,
the *Hail Mary* and the *full of grace*.
Now I have entered the year without words.
I note the queer entrance and the exact voltage.
Without words they exist.
Without words one may touch bread
and be handed bread
and make no sound.

O Mary, tender physician,
come with powders and herbs
for I am in the center.
It is very small and the air is gray
as in a steam house.
I am handed wine as a child is handed milk.
It is presented in a delicate glass
with a round bowl and a thin lip.
The wine itself is pitch-colored, musty and secret.
The glass rises on its own toward my mouth
and I notice this and understand this
only because it has happened.

I have this fear of coughing
but I do not speak,
a fear of rain, a fear of the horseman
who comes riding into my mouth.
The glass tilts in on its own
and I am on fire.
I see two thin streaks burn down my chin.
I see myself as one would see another.
I have been cut in two.

O Mary, open your eyelids.
I am in the domain of silence,
the kingdom of the crazy and the sleeper.
There is blood here
and I have eaten it.
O mother of the womb,
did I come for blood alone?
O little mother,
I am in my own mind.
I am locked in the wrong house.

August 1963

46

MENSTRUATION AT FORTY

I was thinking of a son.
The womb is not a clock
nor a bell tolling,
but in the eleventh month of its life
I feel the November
of the body as well as of the calendar.
In two days it will be my birthday
and as always the earth is done with its harvest.
This time I hunt for death,
the night I lean toward,
the night I want.
Well then —
speak of it!
It was in the womb all along.

I was thinking of a son . . .
You! The never acquired,
the never seeded or unfastened,
you of the genitals I feared,
the stalk and the puppy's breath.
Will I give you my eyes or his?
Will you be the David or the Susan?
(Those two names I picked and listened for.)
Can you be the man your fathers are —
the leg muscles from Michelangelo,
hands from Yugoslavia,
somewhere the peasant, Slavic and determined,
somewhere the survivor, bulging with life —
and could it still be possible,
all this with Susan's eyes?

All this without you —
two days gone in blood.

I myself will die without baptism,
a third daughter they didn't bother.
My death will come on my name day.
What's wrong with the name day?
It's only an angel of the sun.
Woman,
weaving a web over your own,
a thin and tangled poison.
Scorpio,
bad spider —
die!

My death from the wrists,
two name tags,
blood worn like a corsage
to bloom
one on the left and one on the right —
It's a warm room,
the place of the blood.
Leave the door open on its hinges!

Two days for your death
and two days until mine.

Love! That red disease —
year after year, David, you would make me wild!
David! Susan! David! David!
full and disheveled, hissing into the night,
never growing old,
waiting always for you on the porch . . .
year after year,

my carrot, my cabbage,
I would have possessed you before all women,
calling your name,
calling you mine.

November 7, 1963

CHRISTMAS EVE

Oh sharp diamond, my mother!
I could not count the cost
of all your faces, your moods —
that present that I lost.
Sweet girl, my deathbed,
my jewel-fingered lady,
your portrait flickered all night
by the bulbs of the tree.

Your face as calm as the moon
over a mannered sea,
presided at the family reunion,
the twelve grandchildren
you used to wear on your wrist,
a three-months-old baby,
a fat check you never wrote,
the red-haired toddler who danced the twist,
your aging daughters, each one a wife,
each one talking to the family cook,
each one avoiding your portrait,
each one aping your life.

Later, after the party,
after the house went to bed,
I sat up drinking the Christmas brandy,
watching your picture,
letting the tree move in and out of focus.
The bulbs vibrated.
They were a halo over your forehead.
Then they were a beehive,

blue, yellow, green, red;
each with its own juice, each hot and alive
stinging your face. But you did not move.
I continued to watch, forcing myself,
waiting, inexhaustible, thirty-five.

I wanted your eyes, like the shadows
of two small birds, to change.
But they did not age.
The smile that gathered me in, all wit,
all charm, was invincible.
Hour after hour I looked at your face
but I could not pull the roots out of it.
Then I watched how the sun hit
your red sweater, your withered neck,
your badly painted flesh-pink skin.
You who led me by the nose,
I saw you as you were.
Then I thought of your body
as one thinks of murder . . .

Then I said Mary —
Mary, Mary, forgive me
and then I touched a present for the child,
the last I bred before your death;
and then I touched my breast
and then I touched the floor
and then my breast again as if,
somehow, it were one of yours.

December 24, 1963

Black lady,
two eyes,
low as tobacco, who inked you in?
The shoemaker could not do it,
nor the sculptor nor the cubist.
Trunk is what you are, with two washbowls.
You are a sweetener, a drawer of blood — that's all,
a hot voice, an imminence and then a death.
Why death? Death's in the goodbye.

My love,
when you leave in which crevice will you hide?
What signs will remain?
Black slime will not come of it,
nor backwash from the traveler.
You will rest
Like a drowned bat upon my shoulder.
In one hand I will have to hold that silence.
There will be no track anymore.
There will be only that peculiar waiting.
There will be nothing to pick up.
There will be nothing.

There will have been a house —
a house that I knew,
the center of it,
a tiny heart,
synthetic though it was
making that thin buzz-buzz
like a sly beetle.

Black lady,
what will I do
without your two flowers?
I have inhabited you, number by number.
I have pushed you in and out like a needle.
Funny digits, I have danced upon your trunk
and I have knelt on your torso.
With my words I have perjured my soul.
Take note — there will be an absence.
It will be a cancer, spreading like a white dog
who doubles back, not knowing his name.

Although I will inherit darkness
I will keep dialing left to right.
I will struggle like a surgeon.
I will call quickly for the glare of the moon.
I will even dial milk.
I will hold the thread that was fished through the ceiling
that leads to the roof, the pole, the grass,
that ends in the sea.

I will not wait at the rail
looking upon death,
that single stone.
I will call for the boy-child I never had.
I will call like the Jew at the gate.
I will dial the wound over and over
and you will not yield
and there will be nothing,
black lady, nothing,
although I will wait,
unleashed and unheard.

January 3, 1964

WANTING TO DIE

Since you ask, most days I cannot remember.
I walk in my clothing, unmarked by that voyage.
Then the almost unnameable lust returns.

Even then I have nothing against life.
I know well the grass blades you mention,
the furniture you have placed under the sun.

But suicides have a special language.
Like carpenters they want to know *which tools.*
They never ask *why build.*

Twice I have so simply declared myself,
have possessed the enemy, eaten the enemy,
have taken on his craft, his magic.

In this way, heavy and thoughtful,
warmer than oil or water,
I have rested, drooling at the mouth-hole.

I did not think of my body at needle point.
Even the cornea and the leftover urine were gone.
Suicides have already betrayed the body.

Still-born, they don't always die,
but dazzled, they can't forget a drug so sweet
that even children would look on and smile.

To thrust all that life under your tongue! —
that, all by itself, becomes a passion.
Death's a sad bone; bruised, you'd say,

and yet she waits for me, year after year,
to so delicately undo an old wound,
to empty my breath from its bad prison.

Balanced there, suicides sometimes meet,
raging at the fruit, a pumped-up moon,
leaving the bread they mistook for a kiss,

leaving the page of the book carelessly open,
something unsaid, the phone off the hook
and the love, whatever it was, an infection.

February 3, 1964

THE WEDDING NIGHT

There was this time in Boston
before spring was ready — a short celebration —
and then it was over.
I walked down Marlborough Street the day you left me
under branches as tedious as leather,
under branches as stiff as drivers' gloves.
I said, (but only because you were gone)
"Magnolia blossoms have rather a southern sound,
so unlike Boston anyhow,"
and whatever it was that happened, all that pink,
and for so short a time,
was unbelievable, was pinned on.

The magnolias had sat once, each in a pink dress,
looking, of course, at the ceiling.
For weeks the buds had been as sure-bodied
as the twelve-year-old flower girl I was
at Aunt Edna's wedding.
Will they bend, I had asked,
as I walked under them toward you,
bend two to a branch,
cheek, forehead, shoulder to the floor?
I could see that none were clumsy.
I could see that each was tight and firm.
Not one of them had trickled blood —
waiting as polished as gull beaks,
as closed as all that.

I stood under them for nights, hesitating,
and then drove away in my car.

Yet one night in the April night
someone (someone!) kicked each bud open —
to disprove, to mock, to puncture!
The next day they were all hot-colored,
moist, not flawed in fact.
Then they no longer huddled.
They forgot how to hide.
Tense as they had been,
they were flags, gaudy, chafing in the wind.
There was such abandonment in all that!
Such entertainment
in their flaring up.

After that, well —
like faces in a parade,
I could not tell the difference between losing you
and losing them.
They dropped separately after the celebration,
handpicked,
one after the other like artichoke leaves.
After that I walked to my car awkwardly
over the painful bare remains on the brick sidewalk,
knowing that someone had, in one night,
passed roughly through,
and before it was time.

April 27–May 1, 1964

61

LITTLE GIRL, MY STRING BEAN,
MY LOVELY WOMAN

My daughter, at eleven
(almost twelve), is like a garden.

Oh, darling! Born in that sweet birthday suit
and having owned it and known it for so long,
now you must watch high noon enter —
noon, that ghost hour.
Oh, funny little girl — this one under a blueberry sky,
this one! How can I say that I've known
just what you know and just where you are?

It's not a strange place, this odd home
where your face sits in my hand
so full of distance,
so full of its immediate fever.
The summer has seized you,
as when, last month in Amalfi, I saw
lemons as large as your desk-side globe —
that miniature map of the world —
and I could mention, too,
the market stalls of mushrooms
and garlic buds all engorged.
Or I think even of the orchard next door,
where the berries are done
and the apples are beginning to swell.
And once, with our first backyard,
I remember I planted an acre of yellow beans
we couldn't eat.

little fetus, little snail,
carrying a rage, a leftover rage
I cannot undo.

Even a song for your flight
where you fell from the neighbor's tree hut,
where you thought you were walking onto solid blue air,
you thought, *why not?*
and then, you simply left the boards behind
and stepped out into the dust.

O little Icarus,
you chewed on a cloud, you bit the sun
and came tumbling down, head first,
not into the sea, but hard
on the hard packed gravel.
You fell on your eye. You fell on your chin.
What a shiner! What a faint you had
and then crawled home,
a knocked-out humpty dumpty
in my arms.

O humpty-dumpty girl,
I named you Joy.
That's someone's song all by itself.
In the naming of you I named
all things you are . . .
except the ditch
where I left you once,
like an old root that wouldn't take hold,
that ditch where I left you
while I sailed off in madness
over the buildings and under my umbrella,
sailed off for three years
so that the first candle
and the second candle
and the third candle

burned down alone on your birthday cake.
That ditch I want so much to forget
and that you try each day to forget.

Even here in your school portrait
where you repeat third grade,
caught in the need not to grow —
that little prison —
even here you keep up the barrier
with a smile that dies afraid
as it hides your crooked front tooth.
Joy, I call you
and yet your eyes just here
with their shades half-drawn over the gunsights,
over your gigantic knowledge,
over the little blue fish who dart back and forth,
over different streets, the strange rooms,
other people's chairs, other people's food,
ask, "Why was I shut in the cellar?"

And I've got words,
words that dog my heels,
words for sale you might say,
and multiplication cards and cursive writing
that you ignore to teach my fingers
the *cat's cradle* and the *witch's broom.*
Yes! I have instructions before dinner
and hugs after dinner and still those eyes —
away, away,
asking for hymns . . .
without guilt.

And I can only say
a little uncomplicated hymn
is what I wanted to write
and yet I find only your name.

There *was* such a song,
but it's bruised.
It's not mine.

You will jump to it someday
as you will jump out of the pitch of this house.
It will be a holiday, a parade, a fiesta!
Then you'll fly.
You'll really fly.
After that you'll, quite simply, quite calmly
make your own stones, your own floor plan,
your own sound.

I wanted to write such a poem
with such musics, such guitars going;
I tried at the teeth of sound
to draw up such legions of noise;
I tried at the breakwater
to catch the star off each ship;
and at the closing of hands
I looked for their houses
and silences.
I found just one.

      you were mine
      and I lent you out.

I look for uncomplicated hymns
but love has none.

March 1965

YOUR FACE ON THE DOG'S NECK

It is early afternoon.
You sit on the grass
with your rough face on the dog's neck.
Right now
you are both as still as a snapshot.
That infectious dog ought to let a fly bother her,
ought to run out in an immense field,
chasing rabbits and skunks,
mauling the cats, licking insects off her rump,
and stop using you up.
My darling, why do you lean on her so?
I would touch you,
that pulse brooding under your Madras shirt,
each shoulder the most well built house,
the arms, thin birches that do not escape the breeze,
the white teeth that have known me,
that wait at the bottom of the brook
and the tongue, my little fish! . . .
but you are stopped in time.

So I will speak of your eyes
although they are closed.
Tell me, where is each stubborn-colored iris?
Where are the quick pupils that make
the floor tilt under me?
I see only the lids, as tough as riding boots.
Why have your eyes gone into their own room?
Goodnight they are saying
from their little leathery doors.
Or shall I sing of eyes

that have been ruined with mercy and lust
and once with your own death
when you lay bubbling like a caught fish,
sucking on the manufactured oxygen?
Or shall I sing of eyes
that are resting so near the hair
of that hateful animal?
Love twists me, a Spanish flute plays in my blood,
and yet I can see only
your little sleep, an empty place.

But when your eyes open
against the wool stink of her thick hair,
against the faintly sickening neck of that dog,
whom I envy like a thief,
what will I ask?
Will I speak up saying,
there is a hurried song, a certain seizure
from which I gasp?
Or will your eyes lie in wait,
little field mice nestling on their paws?
Perhaps they will say nothing,
perhaps they will be dark and leaden,
having played their own game
somewhere else,
somewhere far off.

Oh, I have learned them and know that
when they open and glance at me
I will turn like a little dancer
and then, quite simply,
and all by myself,
I will fall,
bound to some mother/father,
bound to your sight,
bound for nowhere
and everywhere.

Or, perhaps, my darling,
because it is early afternoon,
I will forget that my voice is full of good people,
forget how my legs could sprawl on the terrace,
forget all that the birds might witness,
the torn dress, the shoes lost in the arbor,
while the neighbor's lawnmower bites and spits out
some new little rows of innocent grass.
Certainly,
I need not speak of it at all.
I will crouch down
and put my cheek near you,
accepting this spayed and flatulent bitch you hold,
letting my face rest in an assembled tenderness
on the old dog's neck.

May 19, 1965

SELF IN 1958

What is reality?
I am a plaster doll; I pose
with eyes that cut open without landfall or nightfall
upon some shellacked and grinning person,
eyes that open, blue, steel, and close.
Am I approximately an I. Magnin transplant?
I have hair, black angel,
black-angel-stuffing to comb,
nylon legs, luminous arms
and some advertised clothes.

I live in a doll's house
with four chairs,
a counterfeit table, a flat roof
and a big front door.
Many have come to such a small crossroad.
There is an iron bed,
(Life enlarges, life takes aim)
a cardboard floor,
windows that flash open on someone's city,
and little more.

Someone plays with me,
plants me in the all-electric kitchen,
Is this what Mrs. Rombauer said?
Someone pretends with me —
I am walled in solid by their noise —
or puts me upon their straight bed.
They think I am me!
Their warmth? Their warmth is not a friend!

They pry my mouth for their cups of gin
and their stale bread.

What is reality
to this synthetic doll
who should smile, who should shift gears,
should spring the doors open in a wholesome disorder,
and have no evidence of ruin or fears?
But I would cry,
rooted into the wall that
was once my mother,
if I could remember how
and if I had the tears.

June 1958–June 1965

SUICIDE NOTE

You speak to me of narcissism but I reply that it is
a matter of my life . . . Artaud

At this time let me somehow bequeath all the leftovers
to my daughters and their daughters . . . Anonymous

Better,
despite the worms talking to
the mare's hoof in the field;
better,
despite the season of young girls
dropping their blood;
better somehow
to drop myself quickly
into an old room.
Better (someone said)
not to be born
and far better
not to be born twice
at thirteen
where the boardinghouse,
each year a bedroom,
caught fire.

Dear friend,
I will have to sink with hundreds of others
on a dumbwaiter into hell.
I will be a light thing.
I will enter death
like someone's lost optical lens.
Life is half enlarged.
The fish and owls are fierce today.
Life tilts backward and forward.
Even the wasps cannot find my eyes.

75

Yes,
eyes that were immediate once.
Eyes that have been truly awake,
eyes that told the whole story —
poor dumb animals.
Eyes that were pierced,
little nail heads,
light blue gunshots.

And once with
a mouth like a cup,
clay colored or blood colored,
open like the breakwater
for the lost ocean
and open like the noose
for the first head.

Once upon a time
my hunger was for Jesus.
O my hunger! My hunger!
Before he grew old
he rode calmly into Jerusalem
in search of death.

This time
I certainly
do not ask for understanding
and yet I hope everyone else
will turn their heads when an unrehearsed fish jumps
on the surface of Echo Lake;
when moonlight,
its bass note turned up loud,
hurts some building in Boston,
when the truly beautiful lie together.
I think of this, surely,
and would think of it far longer

76

if I were not . . . if I were not
at that old fire.

I could admit
that I am only a coward
crying *me me me*
and not mention the little gnats, the moths,
forced by circumstance
to suck on the electric bulb.
But surely you know that everyone has a death,
his own death,
waiting for him.
So I will go now
without old age or disease,
wildly but accurately,
knowing my best route,
carried by that toy donkey I rode all these years,
never asking, "Where are we going?"
We were riding (if I'd only known)
to this.

Dear friend,
please do not think
that I visualize guitars playing
or my father arching his bone.
I do not even expect my mother's mouth.
I know that I have died before —
once in November, once in June.
How strange to choose June again,
so concrete with its green breasts and bellies.
Of course guitars will not play!
The snakes will certainly not notice.
New York City will not mind.
At night the bats will beat on the trees,
knowing it all,
seeing what they sensed all day.

June 1965

77

IN THE BEACH HOUSE

The doors open
and the heat undoes itself,
everyone undoes himself,
everyone walks naked.
Two of them walk on the table.
They are not afraid of God's displeasure.
They will have no truck with the angel
who hoots from the fog horn
and throws the ocean into the rocks outside.
One of them covers the bedstead.
One of them winds round the bedpost
and both of them beat on the floor.

My little cot listens in
all night long —
even with the ocean turned up high,
even with every door boarded up,
they are allowed the lifting of the object,
the placing themselves upon the swing.
Inside my prison of pine and bedspring,
over my window sill, under my knob,
it is plain that they are at
the royal strapping.

Have mercy, little pillow,
stay mute and uncaring,
hear not one word of disaster!
Stay close, little sour feather,
little fellow full of salt.
My loves are oiling their bones

and then delivering them with unspeakable sounds
that carry them this way and that
while summer is hurrying its way in and out,
over and over,
in their room.

July 15, 1965

CRIPPLES AND OTHER STORIES

My doctor, the comedian
I called you every time
and made you laugh yourself
when I wrote this silly rhyme . . .

Each time I give lectures
or gather in the grants
you send me off to boarding school
in training pants.

God damn it, father-doctor.
I'm really thirty-six.
I see dead rats in the toilet.
I'm one of the lunatics.

Disgusted, mother put me
on the potty. She was good at this.
My father was fat on scotch.
It leaked from every orifice.

Oh the enemas of childhood,
reeking of outhouses and shame!
Yet you rock me in your arms
and whisper my nickname.

Or else you hold my hand
and teach me love too late.
And that's the hand of the arm
they tried to amputate.

Though I was almost seven
I was an awful brat.
I put it in the Easy Wringer.
It came out nice and flat.

I was an instant cripple
from my finger to my shoulder.
The laundress wept and swooned.
My mother had to hold her.

I knew I was a cripple.
Of course, I'd known it from the start.
My father took the crowbar
and broke that wringer's heart.

The surgeons shook their heads.
They really didn't know —
Would the cripple inside of me
be a cripple that would show?

My father was a perfect man,
clean and rich and fat.
My mother was a brilliant thing.
She was good at that.

You hold me in your arms.
How strange that you're so tender!
Child-woman that I am,
you think that you can mend her.

As for the arm,
unfortunately it grew.
Though mother said a withered arm
would put me in *Who's Who*.

For years she described it.
She sang it like a hymn.

By then she loved the shrunken thing,
my little withered limb.

My father's cells clicked each night,
intent on making money.
And as for my cells, they brooded,
little queens, on honey.

On boys too, as a matter of fact,
and cigarettes and cars.
Mother frowned at my wasted life.
My father smoked cigars.

My cheeks blossomed with maggots.
I picked at them like pearls.
I covered them with pancake.
I wound my hair in curls.

My father didn't know me
but you kiss me in my fever.
My mother knew me twice
and then I had to leave her.

But those are just two stories
and I have more to tell
from the outhouse, the greenhouse
where you draw me out of hell.

Father, I'm thirty-six,
yet I lie here in your crib.
I'm getting born again, Adam,
as you prod me with your rib.

October 1965

PAIN FOR A DAUGHTER

Blind with love, my daughter
has cried nightly for horses,
those long-necked marchers and churners
that she has mastered, any and all,
reigning them in like a circus hand —
the excitable muscles and the ripe neck;
tending this summer, a pony and a foal.
She who is too squeamish to pull
a thorn from the dog's paw,
watched her pony blossom with distemper,
the underside of the jaw swelling
like an enormous grape.
Gritting her teeth with love,
she drained the boil and scoured it
with hydrogen peroxide until pus
ran like milk on the barn floor.

Blind with loss all winter,
in dungarees, a ski jacket and a hard hat,
she visits the neighbors' stable,
our acreage not zoned for barns;
they who own the flaming horses
and the swan-whipped thoroughbred
that she tugs at and cajoles,
thinking it will burn like a furnace
under her small-hipped English seat.

Blind with pain she limps home.
The thoroughbred has stood on her foot.
He rested there like a building.

He grew into her foot until they were one.
The marks of the horseshoe printed
into her flesh, the tips of her toes
ripped off like pieces of leather,
three toenails swirled like shells
and left to float in blood in her riding boot.

Blind with fear, she sits on the toilet,
her foot balanced over the washbasin,
her father, hydrogen peroxide in hand,
performing the rites of the cleansing.
She bites on a towel, sucked in breath,
sucked in and arched against the pain,
her eyes glancing off me where
I stand at the door, eyes locked
on the ceiling, eyes of a stranger,
and then she cries . . .
Oh my God, help me!
Where a child would have cried *Mama!*
Where a child would have believed *Mama!*
she bit the towel and called on God
and I saw her life stretch out . . .
I saw her torn in childbirth,
and I saw her, at that moment,
in her own death and I knew that she
knew.

November 1965

THE ADDICT

Sleepmonger,
deathmonger,
with capsules in my palms each night,
eight at a time from sweet pharmaceutical bottles
I make arrangements for a pint-sized journey.
I'm the queen of this condition.
I'm an expert on making the trip
and now they say I'm an addict.
Now they ask why.
Why!

Don't they know
that I promised to die!
I'm keeping in practice.
I'm merely staying in shape.
The pills are a mother, but better,
every color and as good as sour balls.
I'm on a diet from death.

Yes, I admit
it has gotten to be a bit of a habit —
blows eight at a time, socked in the eye,
hauled away by the pink, the orange,
the green and the white goodnights.
I'm becoming something of a chemical
mixture.
That's it!

My supply
of tablets
has got to last for years and years.

I like them more than I like me.
Stubborn as hell, they won't let go.
It's a kind of marriage.
It's a kind of war
where I plant bombs inside
of myself.

Yes
I try
to kill myself in small amounts,
an innocuous occupation.
Actually I'm hung up on it.
But remember I don't make too much noise.
And frankly no one has to lug me out
and I don't stand there in my winding sheet.
I'm a little buttercup in my yellow nightie
eating my eight loaves in a row
and in a certain order as in
the laying on of hands
or the black sacrament.

It's a ceremony
but like any other sport
it's full of rules.
It's like a musical tennis match where
my mouth keeps catching the ball.
Then I lie on my altar
elevated by the eight chemical kisses.

What a lay me down this is
with two pink, two orange,
two green, two white goodnights.
Fee-fi-fo-fum —
Now I'm borrowed.
Now I'm numb.

First of February 1966

LIVE

Live or die, but don't poison everything . . .

Well, death's been here
for a long time —
it has a hell of a lot
to do with hell
and suspicion of the eye
and the religious objects
and how I mourned them
when they were made obscene
by my dwarf-heart's doodle.
The chief ingredient
is mutilation.
And mud, day after day,
mud like a ritual,
and the baby on the platter,
cooked but still human,
cooked also with little maggots,
sewn onto it maybe by somebody's mother,
the damn bitch!

Even so,
I kept right on going on,
a sort of human statement,
lugging myself as if
I were a sawed-off body
in the trunk, the steamer trunk.
This became a perjury of the soul.
It became an outright lie
and even though I dressed the body
it was still naked, still killed.
It was caught

in the first place at birth,
like a fish.
But I played it, dressed it up,
dressed it up like somebody's doll.
Is life something you play?
And all the time wanting to get rid of it?
And further, everyone yelling at you
to shut up. And no wonder!
People don't like to be told
that you're sick
and then be forced
to watch
you
come
down with the hammer.

Today life opened inside me like an egg
and there inside
after considerable digging
I found the answer.
What a bargain!
There was the sun,
her yolk moving feverishly,
tumbling her prize —
and you realize that she does this daily!
I'd known she was a purifier
but I hadn't thought
she was solid,
hadn't known she was an answer.
God! It's a dream,
lovers sprouting in the yard
like celery stalks
and better,
a husband straight as a redwood,
two daughters, two sea urchins,
picking roses off my hackles.

If I'm on fire they dance around **it**
and cook marshmallows.
And if I'm ice
they simply skate on me
in little ballet costumes.

Here,
all along,
thinking I was a killer,
anointing myself daily
with my little poisons.
But no.
I'm an empress.
I wear an apron.
My typewriter writes.
It didn't break the way it warned.
Even crazy, I'm as nice
as a chocolate bar.
Even with the witches' gymnastics
they trust my incalculable city,
my corruptible bed.

O dearest three,
I make a soft reply.
The witch comes on
and you paint her pink.
I come with kisses in my hood
and the sun, the smart one,
rolling in my arms.
So I say *Live*
and turn my shadow three times round
to feed our puppies as they come,
the eight Dalmatians we didn't drown,
despite the warnings: The abort! The destroy!
Despite the pails of water that waited
to drown them, to pull them down like stones,

they came, each one headfirst,
blowing bubbles the color of cataract-blue
and fumbling for the tiny tits.
Just last week, eight Dalmatians,
¾ of a lb., lined up like cord wood
each
like a
birch tree.
I promise to love more if they come,
because in spite of cruelty
and the stuffed railroad cars for the ovens,
I am not what I expected. Not an Eichmann.
The poison just didn't take.
So I won't hang around in my hospital shift,
repeating The Black Mass and all of it.
I say *Live, Live* because of the sun,
the dream, the excitable gift.

February the last, 1966